Into The Nothingness

Poems of Time & Measure

Agantuk (Pratiti Nath)

BookLeaf
Publishing
India | USA | UK

Made with ❤ on the BookLeaf Publishing Platform
www.bookleafpub.in
www.bookleafpub.com

Dedication

To all who -
Reads and thinks
And thinks and acts.
In between the place
Called Life.

Preface

Dear readers,

This book is an entourage of people and places
Strangers, colleagues and friends,
All who have come and gone
Leaving a delicate fabric of realisations.
Some of them are old
Some are new
Whatever it is - boon or bane
I leave it to you.

Sincerely,
Agantuk (Pratiti Nath)
A poet - lost and found in an editor.
From Somewhere in Calcutta.

Acknowledgements

People are stories to tell
And songs you forget,
You have to rewind the radio
From time to time.
This is a token of appreciation
For all who I have met
And got to observe and learn,
Especially those I was born of
And those who inspired.
From the Beatles to Michael Caine
To my parents and penfriend in the UK
To my muse.
Thank you for
Letting the Beat Go On

Agantuk (Pratiti Nath)
Somewhere In Calcutta.

1. The Tree

There was once a tree as old as me,
That grew from some seeds
Seeds that never germinated.
Like me, it never travelled
Untouched by love
Unwithered by death
It stood forever.

There was once a tree as old as me,
That lay at the edge
The edge of the city and the forest.
Like me, it grew past the memory
Unperturbed by grief
Unwished by belief
It stood forever.

There was once a tree as old as me,
That lived in the in-betweens.
There was once a tree as old as me,

That never longed for the greens.
There was once a tree as old as me.

.

2. A Flower Forgotten in Time

Broken lives, meandering smiles
Idioms stitched in a haywire.
Times fail, but the human trails,
Clear sky and an open mind.
A flower long forgotten.

An emperor of a crown or a troubled flower seller?
Hither and thither he shouts,
Sometimes crawling in a busy market space,
Sometimes borrowing from a dream.
Flowers or dreams?
What he sells?

A meal for an empty stomach at large,
A dying body at the dumping yard.
A broken leg, an empty stomach, and a watchful eye
Is all that's there in his home?
It doesn't speak of flowers or dreams.
It reeks of sustenance, an undue existence.

A forgetful society, harrowing times and powerful lords
That neither chimes nor rhymes.

Sunflowers, roses, marigolds?
What's the flower that bears the strength of all? They
ask.
The strength to bury time as a foe
Or is it just a petunia that bore?
They demand, and he supplies
But where's his supply?
It's buried in the hope of another time.
Still, the brokenness climbs, treads the busy lanes.
A flower forgotten in time.

3. Notre Dame

A spendthrift night toils hour by hour.
A time that spells a kingdom of doom,
Where the gargoyles chime one by one.
First, they rhyme, then they cry
For a crime has unfolded in the dome.

A rage of decent,
An agony of the crescent,
The air goes wild with the melody of dissent.
The spire fumes and the bell towers wonder,
Of a place that's no longer.

As they pass one by one,
The colours assimilate, giving a hope,
For hunchback of Notre Dame takes refuge,
In a chasm of "Au Revoir".

4. April Came

April came with the belief
That the delusions are part of the self.
As you set to know her
She behaves like an absconding flower.
Day and night, she eludes your garden
Only to give away to your haunted guardian.

She has a mistaken look
That your illusions partook.
A jostled head
Upside-down eyes in place of a blabbering mouth
instead.
Her scary hollow eyes
Gives away to the injuries done by a knife.
April is the one to understand
A depression you carry in disguise of a flower stand.

She made you wonder by the night
Sleepless and fragile in everyone's sight.
April came to you

As you are in need of the cue.
April bore the reach fruits of your troubled past
April is here to last.

April came to ascertain
Yours is one of those mental illness to be certain.
Of anxiety, depression, insomnia, dementia she smells
April tells everyone's tale.
April is here to make you belong
To those numerous she throng.
April is your story to tell
April came to bring you out of the shell.

5. When Death Came Visiting

I couldn't wait for him
So he crept into my being.
Together we started walking.
We passed the baffled crowd sobbing.

Next, we stopped at the synagogue
To hear the verse of a grieving mother.
By the river, we witnessed a rotten carcass.
A queer being survived by his purpose.
Two yards down the line,
there were lovers by the moonshine.
As we passed the river,
We saw a lonely child quiver.

At the helm of death
They all bequeath.
As they refuse to wait for him
He creeps into them.

Death is thy name
Comes to visit without shame.

6. The Morning After A Failed Suicide

The morning after a failed suicide
The world starts to haunt.
It reminds of all broken joints
And the things you couldn't decide.
The houses in the neighbourhood change
And you try to hide from a new neighbour in vain.

The morning after a failed suicide
You wake up to try again.
The hand by your bedside has gone in pain
While you were busy with the life of pride.
The memories start to flash out
As you remember the lies you told yourself.

The morning after a failed suicide
You recollect the taste of your better half,
The evening meals where you laughed
While she shone bright with a love one can't hide.
As you walk past the neighbourhood with a smile

A cat stands by guarding you with fright.

The morning after a failed suicide
The world tries to rescue you from your plight
A bunch of kids and a clown with a 1964 mint edition
quarter.

7. Whose House Is It?

Whose house is it? I ask.
Are you deserted like the summer afternoon?
With memories of children playing
And murdered relations.

Did you play with the dawn and dusk?
Of a thousand splendid suns
And sordid affairs.
Have you plied through the edges of history?
Alone and forlorn
A mistress sang in your courtyard
And the rioters booked the coffin guards.

Whose house is it? I ask
Are you the ones who plague my dream?
Alone, tranquil and bereft
An undeciphered language you speak.
Streaming of deadly laughter and silent sorrows
Are you the one for me?
Whose house is it?

8. I Know Why It Rains

I know why it rains
When there's a sun over the horizon.
It has buried the pains
Of engulfing a dreadful poison.
Of the acres of land we had,
Couldn't provide the clothes that clad.

Now each day's harvest
Lies in the distance travelled between successive rests.
I know why it rains,
It speaks of a story that pains.

I know why it rains
When there's very little to gain.
I know why it rains.
Refugees are the cloud
That comes down as rain.

9. The Rain That Was

The rain that clears vision.
The rain that makes love every time it falls.
In foggy morning light,
Amidst misty twilight.
The rain that makes you fall in love.
The unknown passerby's song,
The quarrelsome midnight feud.

The rain that makes the poet write in monosyllables.
Of words of frosty winter night,
Of someone's frail eyesight.
The rain that makes you sad when you drench alone.
Of long-travelled past,
Twirling alleys of famished dust.

The rain that sleeps as a little bemoaning kid.
Tired of each day's foul play,
of building sandcastles every way.
The rain that rests in the crematorium by the night.

Only to wake up at the voices of fright.
The rain that will be again.

10. There's Something About June

There's something about June.
The way she dresses night and noon,
Of sultry garnishes and drowsing rain by the day.
Celestial events peeping behind the clouds in the
evening sky,
Whispering of unrelinquishing love of a summer lad and
a winter lass.

There's something about June.
The way she speaks of a danger in the loom,
of torrential rains and inundated plains.

There's something about June.
The way she whistles night and noon,
Of monologues of musical ballads of a lost traveller.

There's something about June,
Which makes you write even in gloom.

There's something about June
Which reminds of Frost on a monsoon afternoon.

11. Think Of Me

Think of me when you are weary.
Of travelling an exhausting path.
When you see the birds resting,
When you sigh over failures,
When you despair in unforeseen pain.

Think of me when you see the setting sun.
Hiding behind the caved windows.
When the last leaf falls,
When you play your ballad.

Think of me in your last whistle,
In your dying moments.
Whether in tenderness or bitterness,
In joy or in despair.

Think of me when your heart longs.
For I loved you late, but I loved well.
Loved you with my all.

12. The Face of Exploration

The face of exploration often remains unknown
Seldom revealing where you've grown.
Sometimes you crash, sometimes you land
In the end, all that matters - what have you learned?
The weather that will change over the years
The dust storms that will eat up the crops.
Most won't realise what you bore
How you can tame the hunger of a civilisation that
galore.

Then one by one they sit on the throne
Until everyone gets to groan.
Some will get to the temples and churches
Some will bear it with headaches
While you make your way over the ages.

Time after time, you will remind
What's in the sea and in the air
That we must mind
There's not very much time for us to wear.

We are waiting the world to tear
Forgetting it doesn't live in fear.
It goes on to the horizon there
When you and I are no longer here.

13. H O M E

The neighbourhood looks sombre today.
It's troubled friend lied bereft from the day.
The man of the festivals begins the festival in silence.
As his long time partner has gone before him.
A week before the onset of the autumnal festivities
And a day that calls every woman to her abode,
His better half has gone home.

The septuagenarian lay empty in bed.
Listening to the ambulance sound
Getting marred by the drums of the festival.
He was never a good keeper of time.

Although he was the cashier of the festival committee.
Time and money are not the same thing he felt,
Both are essential to live
But life takes the one that is most valued.
For those who ails like him go last
While the able bodied go first.

14. Long Ago

We parted long ago,
Long from the time of despair,
That holds us naively together.
We parted long ago, You and I,
Long from the time spent walking on the grass.
The morning dew has dried up in the sun
And the afternoon has grown weary.
The summers of youth are gone
And along with it, the pale white winters.

Everything is autumn now.
Everything is fragile.
They hardly wake up
And they always fall.
Some from a distance where I can't catch them,
Some very near where I am not present.
All of them speak without uttering a word.
All have buried a bloodied sword.
We parted long ago, You and I.
Long from the time you were you

And I was I.

It always smells of rain and mud now.
But no one is walking to the bank anymore.
The post office has long gone out of business.
It's only just the two of us burning our pensions.
No one writes a letter to anyone now.
I know I wrote to you a long ago,
But I have spent all my monsoons writing to you.
Always by your grave
And never on your bedside.

We parted long ago – You and I.
Long before we met.
Long before we were born,
And we continued parting at each day's end.
Only to find out that we were living in the same house.

15. The Window

Once I had a window
It had a small flower opening
One by one, it blossomed
Sometimes into a road not taken
Sometimes into the sound of rain.

Some of it whined and creaked
Its lover has gone to a different shore
A letter comes in by post once a year.
At others, it wonders of birds.
Where have the sparrows gone?
The Robins were a bad omen
But they often filled her cavern.

Where have the songs gone?
Half of it seems like a lost tune,
The other half smells of rain and dune.
The window no longer creaks
It's made of stern erratic glass now.
One that restricts sounds

One that abolishes the clowns.
The Window never opens now.

16. It's Only Yesterday

It's only yesterday
Even if it is long years ago
Long years since you first woke up
To your mother humming by the window.
Long years since you first heard of war
Of men and women coming and going.

It's only yesterday
Even if it is months ago.
Months since you first saw your child
playing with the pebbles on the road from school.
Months since the milkman quarrelled
On his way to every house in the neighbourhood.

It's only yesterday
Even if it is weeks ago.
Weeks since you last visited your lover
And gave her a goodbye kiss.
Weeks since the tree by the window kept you warm
On cold, lonely, distraught nights.

It's only yesterday
Even if it is days ago.
Days since you had a full meal
Days since you had a sound sleep
Days since you sang your last song.
Days since you saw a film
Days since you were part of a story.

It's only yesterday
When it all ended and started again.
The beginning of a beautiful ending.

17. To Dickie, The Bird That Stayed

"When Dickie says you're out, you're out," they say
But for people growing up on your story, it was your say.
A 7-year-old girl was bold by your jovialness.
The humble miner's son, who was congenial
The man who was the "gentle" in the gentleman's game.

An eccentricity and earnestness
That reminded of typical Indian uncles in gully cricket.
From the quirkiness in matches on telly
To the endearing story of friendship on YouTube,
You gave a hope of what it was like to be earnest.
What it was like—
To have no barriers in mind
And give it back to the people you belong to.

From a 7-year-old to a 36-year-old now
I wish your values stand the test of time
And in this age of divided people
A friendship like Parky, Dickie and Boycott

Build up communities for generations to come.

18. Language

Once you were the voice of a mother,
Valiant proclamation of a lover.
Withered walls have forgotten words,
In their dwellings hang bloodied swords.

A solitary savage woman utters thy name.
Few are left to stem them.
Language you are a necessity still.
For linguistics to decipher a buried civilisation
underneath.

Language, an expression of our will,
That changes according to times still.
Language, remembers her dying siblings,
Language that remains, a mother as long as we speak.

Language, uttered in times of sigh and pain;
Of untold griefs and solitary sorrows.
Language, the shape of our thoughts;
Without you, we are abstract beings.

Language separates us from the rest.
Language that make us human beings.

19. I Am

I am the crippled fingers clenched as a fist to pray.
I am the frail hand that never betrays.
I am the voice chanting at a grave.
I am the tomorrow that never came.

I am the moon of a planet.
I am the hymn from your clarinet.
I am the night you slept.
I am the darkness that left.

I am the gap between seconds.
I am the coffin that beckons.
I am the memory you forget.
I am the remembrance that you regret.

I am the love unloved.
I am the friendship that you forged.
I am the river bed underneath
I am the undying death.

20. Sixty-Nine

Of your sixty-nine,
We are a little over the line.
In your nascent days,
We were there to stay.

Since you've learned to walk,
We've learnt to talk.
Seldom do we fray,
Into the narrow alley where you stay.
On your sixty-nine,
We proclaim to be thine.
Throughout the year,
we seldom remember the line.

Of your sixty-nine,
I have hardly called you mine.
Of your sixty-nine,
I have barely known you nine.
Of my twenty-four,
I have known you all the more.

But, on your sixty-nine;
I would proudly call you mine.

21. We Will Meet Again

When memories fade
And defiant hands try to escape –
When you long for a friend
In trying times that do not end.
We will meet again.

In the land of forget-me-nots
Where memory plays its have-nots –
In between the spaces
Where time slows down its pace,
We will meet again.

At the junction of wordplay
Where conjunctions and adjectives forfeit their play.
We will meet again.
We will meet again.

www.ingramcontent.com/pod-product-compliance
Lightning Source LLC
Chambersburg PA
CBHW050954030426
42339CB00007B/382